Character
and
Courage

A Mentor's Message in 1 and 2 Timothy

Lifeway Press®
Brentwood, Tennessee

ISBN 978-1-0877-6729-1
Item 005838134
Dewey Decimal Classification Number: 242
Subject Heading: DEVOTIONAL LITERATURE / BIBLE STUDY AND TEACHING / GOD

Printed in the United States of America

Student Ministry Publishing
Lifeway Resources
200 Powell Place, Suite 100
Brentwood, TN, 37027-7707

We believe that the Bible has God for its author; salvation for its end; and truth, without any mixture of error, for its matter and that all Scripture is totally true and trustworthy. To review Lifeway's doctrinal guideline, please visit www.lifeway.com/doctrinalguideline.

publishing team

Director, Student Ministry
Ben Trueblood

Manager, Student Ministry Publishing
John Paul Basham

Editorial Team Leader
Karen Daniel

Writer
Mike Lovato

Content Editor
Kyle Wiltshire

Production Editors
April-Lyn Caouette
Stephanie Cross

Graphic Designer
Shiloh Stufflebeam

Table of Contents

Intro

What do *Star Wars*, *Lord of the Rings*, and *Harry Potter*, all have in common? They are all versions of the classic "hero's journey" found in many stories over time. In each of these stories we find similar elements. There's the unlikely hero, like Harry Potter, Luke Skywalker, or Frodo. There are the sidekicks, like Ron and Hermione, Han Solo and Chewbacca, and Samwise. There's the comic relief, like C-3PO and R2-D2 or Merry and Pippin. There's the quest the hero must take, like destroying the Death Star or carrying the one ring to Mount Doom. On the quest, the hero needs someone to guide them—a mentor. Enter Dumbledore, Obi Wan Kenobi, and Gandalf. Without the mentors, the heroes wouldn't get far.

As Christians we are not on a hero's journey—Jesus is the hero, and He completed the quest by dying on the cross and being raised from the dead! But we do need mentors. Every single one of us—whether we've been a Christian for six minutes, six months, six years, or six decades—needs a mentor. We need someone who has been following Jesus longer than we have and can come alongside us, invest in our lives, and help us as we follow Him. Jesus might have finished the quest, but we are on a journey to grow in our faith and become more like Him.

Can you imagine if one of the most prolific writers of the New Testament offered to be your mentor? Imagine if you could sit down and hear his stories and learn from his mistakes. Imagine if you could ask him questions about the amazing things he saw God do and learn how to walk closer with Jesus. Guess what? We don't have to imagine it. The apostle Paul wrote two letters to a person, who wasn't much older than you, named Timothy. Paul was Timothy's mentor, and in these two letters he does all of this and more. Thankfully, we have copies of these letters, and we can read their contents and apply their truths to our lives.

In 1 and 2 Timothy, we find a mentor's message to his student. His message is not some distant, unattainable musing on things we can't relate to. His message is simple: God desires for us to be people of character and courage. For the next thirty days, take advantage of the opportunity to sit at the feet of one of the greatest mentors you could ever have and learn the message he gave to his student.

Getting Started

*This devotional contains thirty days of content, broken down into sections. Each day is divided into three elements—**discover**, **delight**, and **display**—to help you grow in your faith.*

discover

This section helps you examine the passage in light of who God is and determine what it says about your identity in relationship to Him. Included here is the daily Scripture reading and key verses, along with illustrations and commentary to guide you as you learn more about God's Word.

delight

In this section, you'll be challenged by questions and activities that help you see how God is alive and active in every detail of His Word and your life.

display

Here's where you take action. This section calls you to apply what you've learned through each day.

Each day also includes a prayer activity at the conclusion of the devotion.

Throughout the devotional, you'll also find extra items to help you connect with the topic personally, such as Scripture memory verses, additional resources, and interactive articles.

CHARACTER

Character is who we are—not who we want others to think we are or who we want to be. The good thing about character is that it can be developed, shaped, and changed. Mentors can help us grow in our character, which is what Paul did for Timothy in this first letter. Paul and his letters were both filled with wisdom and advice. He wrote to help his young student know how to be a person of good character in good times and through times of struggle.

Mentor Me

discover

READ 1 TIMOTHY 1:1-2.

Paul, an apostle of Christ Jesus by the command of God our Savior and of Christ Jesus our hope: To Timothy, my true son in the faith. Grace, mercy, and peace from God the Father and Christ Jesus our Lord.
— 1 Timothy 1:1-2

Mentors are people who help us in different ways. A mentor might help someone with an area of schooling or maybe with getting better at a sport. A mentor is at least a little further down the road than you and is able to assist you in your progress. As a Christian, though, the most important mentors you can ever have are the ones who will invest in your walk with Jesus and help you grow in your faith.

Timothy had an incredible mentor in the apostle Paul. Paul was an early church leader who had met Jesus in a powerful way, planted churches all over the place, and wrote much of the New Testament we have today. Timothy was a young pastor who had learned all about the Scriptures from a very young age and was set up with an incredible foundation of faith.

Paul saw potential in Timothy as a leader, so he brought him along on his journeys. They spent time together encouraging and equipping churches in various towns, and we see the result of this partnership in Acts 16:5 which says, "So the churches were strengthened in the faith and grew daily in numbers."

delight

What do you think it means that Paul referred to Timothy as his "true son in the faith"?

How do you think Timothy might have found value from being mentored by Paul?

Character and Courage

display

There's a pretty big chance that you've had some people in your life who have helped your faith become what it is today. Take a minute to list the names of people who have invested in your walk with Jesus. Reflect on how they have helped you grow spiritually. Pick one of the people who has invested in you and find a way to thank them for that investment. You might send them a text, tell them face-to-face how they've helped you, or even drop a card in the mail.

Spend some time in prayer focused on three aspects of mentors today. First, thank God for the mentors He has brought into your life. Second, ask God to help you see new lessons you can be learning from these people. Finally, ask God if He might want you to mentor someone who's a little bit spiritually younger than you are.

The Main Goal

discover

READ 1 TIMOTHY 1:3-11.

Now the goal of our instruction is love that comes from a pure heart, a good conscience, and a sincere faith.
— 1 Timothy 1:5

Paul sought to help Timothy fully understand how to best lead the church. Paul had seen how easy it is for people to get caught up in talking about things that may seem spiritual but, at best, don't really matter or, at worst, are actually untrue. He wanted Timothy to keep the main thing the main thing.

What is the main goal for Timothy and others in church leadership? The goal is ultimately love. We often think of love as a feeling or maybe even always connected to romance. The biblical love Paul was writing about has three key characteristics. First, it comes from a pure heart. Biblical love is about our motives not just our actions. Second, it comes from a good conscience. It's much simpler to love people well when we are fully living life God's way. Third, it comes from a sincere faith. Many today view love as something disconnected from truth. The fact of the matter is love must be rooted in the full truth of the gospel or it simply isn't what God intends for it to be.

The goal of teaching is never just to get more information. It's designed to transform us through Jesus's love and to help us love others well.

delight

Why do you think people can get distracted by conversations that don't really matter instead of focusing on the biblical truth?

How can instruction or learning the Bible help people develop ways of loving others better?

display

Think through the three areas Paul wrote about in verse 5 that are the sources of the love he was aiming to see among believers. A pure heart has good motives. A good conscience is living honestly before God. A sincere faith understands and believes in the gospel. Reflect on each of these areas. Would you say your heart is pure? Is your conscience clear before God? How sincere is your faith in the gospel? We all have room to grow in each of these areas. Pick one and seek to grow in it today.

In your time of prayer, ask God to give you a full focus on Him as you study His Word regularly. Pray that He would help you leave times of Bible study with a greater love for Him and for others. Ask Him to show you specifically how you can display love better.

Character and Courage

DAY 3

An Unlikely Leader

discover

READ 1 TIMOTHY 1:12-17.

But I received mercy for this reason, so that in me, the worst of them, Christ Jesus might demonstrate his extraordinary patience as an example to those who would believe in him for eternal life.
— 1 Timothy 1:16

Imagine the first years of the early church, just getting its start after Jesus ascended to heaven. People were repenting of their sin and believing in the gospel. There were many new believers to be discipled and plenty of people around who needed to know Jesus. This would require strong leaders. In fact, would require several strong leaders.

One of those strong early church leaders was Paul. But if you were on the leadership selection committee of the early church, you probably wouldn't have picked Paul. I mean, this guy had been full of arrogance, blasphemy (speaking disrespectfully of God), and actually persecuted Christians by hunting them down and having them put to death. He doesn't seem like the ideal leader God would use to start churches, strengthen believers, and write much of the New Testament. How can someone go from where Paul began to where Paul ended up?

God is full of mercy and can use absolutely anyone to accomplish His purposes. Paul might have seemed like a strange selection, but God is in the business of taking unlikely people and empowering them to do exactly what He wants them to do.

delight

Paul called himself, "the worst of them." What are some reasons Paul would call himself by this title?

How does the selection of Paul as a leader in the early church give hope to others who might not think they're worthy of God's love?

display

There are two big takeaways from today's passage. First, you can celebrate the fact that God wants to use you, no matter what you've done in the past. You're never too far gone to be used by God. Be encouraged that He wants to use you! Second, there are probably people in your life that you might think would simply never come to faith in Jesus, let alone be used by Him in leadership. They might seem too angry, too sinful, or too proud—but these are the very people Christ gave His life for. Look for opportunities to show His love to people like this, because you never know what God has in store for them!

Pray today that God would open your eyes to people in your life who need to know Jesus. Pray specifically that He would help you have a heart for people you might think would not be very open to the gospel. Ask God to show you in a fresh way that no one is ever beyond His reach. Ask Him to prepare you to step through the doors of opportunity He opens for you.

Prayer is the Battle

discover

READ 1 TIMOTHY 1:18–2:7.

First of all, then, I urge that petitions, prayers, intercessions, and thanksgivings be made for everyone.
— 1 Timothy 2:1

"All we can do now is pray." Have you ever heard this, thought this, or said it yourself? Sometimes we act as if prayer is our last resort. We try every strategy and give every effort, and when those don't seem to be working, we finally call on God to act in the situation. This is certainly not what Paul taught about prayer.

Paul told Timothy to fight the good fight. The very first instruction he gave Timothy for battle was prayer. Paul encouraged Timothy that all types of prayers are to be made for everyone, and then Paul challenged Timothy to pray for kings and those in authority specifically. By faithfully becoming a person of prayer, Timothy's prayer life would pave the way for believers to live in peace and have the best possible opportunity to share the gospel with others.

Verses 5 and 6 highlight the importance of these prayers. They're all designed to help point people to Jesus, the one and only way to the one and only God. Jesus gave His life so all could come to know Him and experience the saving relationship He offers. Prayer clears the battlefield for evangelism.

delight

What are your first thoughts when you read about Paul telling Timothy to "fight the good fight" (1:18)?

What do verses 5 and 6 tell you about God and Jesus?

display

It can be scary to talk to your friends about the gospel. You might be afraid they'll ask a question and you won't know the answer. You might be afraid they won't take you seriously because of mistakes they've seen you make. You might even be afraid they won't want to be friends with you anymore.

Fighting the battle of prayer isn't a one hundred percent guarantee that all your fears will disappear, but it is vital to your efforts to see your friends and family come to know Jesus. Start simple by making a list of three friends who don't know Christ. Commit to pray for them by name every single day. Then look for opportunities to share the gospel with them as God leads.

Your prayer time today can be the beginning of this process of praying regularly for your lost friends. Ask God to reveal names of people you should be praying for daily. Ask Him to increase your love for these people. Finally, ask God for courage to fight the good fight as you seek to help these people come to know Him.

Character and Courage

The Right Focus

discover

READ 1 TIMOTHY 2:8-15.

**Therefore I want the men everywhere to pray, lifting
up holy hands without anger or disputing.**
— 1 Timothy 2:8

We live in a world that's pretty obsessed with calling attention to ourselves. Don't believe me? Just think about social media for a moment. It can quickly become a place filled with content that's all about how people will respond to it. We can easily become people who are all about getting more likes, more comments, and more followers. This isn't the life meant for a Christ-follower though. Paul gives some specific instructions to men and women in this passage that we can all learn from.

Paul challenges men to focus on prayer. It's tough to maintain a healthy prayer life if you're holding on to anger or arguments with other people. So, Paul tells Timothy to instruct men to pray with holy hands lifted up, not hands that are constantly ready for a fight.

Paul challenges women to focus on modesty and good works. Modesty here is about pointing attention to God instead of self. Clothing and makeup aren't sinful in and of themselves, but if we get ourselves in a mindset that uses those things to bring attention to ourselves, we've missed the point.

Simply put: both men and women are to be concerned with living lives of good character that consistently point others to God instead of themselves.

delight

Why do you think Paul advised men toward things that lead them away from anger?

Why do you think Paul advised women toward things that led them away from a focus on their personal appearance?

Why is it better to keep the focus on God and not ourselves?

display

Today's passage gives an opportunity to do some self-evaluation, whether you're a guy or a girl. Here are some questions you might use to help evaluate your life. Is your life defined by godly character or worldly character? Are there any conflicts in your relationships with others that might be blocking your prayer life? Is your outward appearance distracting you and others from keeping the proper attention and focus on God alone?

Those questions may raise up areas of life that need some adjustments. You might want to ask a godly friend or leader at church to help you walk through changes that need to be made in your life.

In your prayer time, submit your motives and desires to God. Ask Him to bring peace to your relationships. Ask Him to grow your prayer life as He grows your character. Submit your outward appearance to God and seek to consistently keep the focus on Him alone.

Character Matters

discover

READ 1 TIMOTHY 3:1-13.

**This saying is trustworthy: "If anyone aspires to
be an overseer, he desires a noble work."
— 1 Timothy 3:1**

Leadership always requires higher standards. Think about this even in terms of your teachers at school. They need to know more about the subject they are teaching and they need to live at a higher level of maturity than you. Leaders are always seeking to take their followers on a journey, and they can't take them on that journey if they've not walked the path themselves.

Paul gives lists of qualifications for two offices in the church: overseer (or pastor) and deacon. The lists are nearly identical except the overseer must also be able to teach. All the other qualities mentioned on these lists really have nothing to do with ability and everything to do with character. Paul was challenging Timothy to only select leaders who have this type of godly character.

Character is the most important qualification for leadership. The reality is we all learn a lot about what it means to follow Jesus by watching the lives of our leaders. Paul knew this to be true and put a huge emphasis on the character of those who would be leading God's church.

delight

Why should the list of qualifications for overseers and deacons be so similar to each other?

Why was the reputation of these leaders to outsiders so important?

display

You might be tempted to quickly skim today's passage and move on because you are neither a pastor nor a deacon and you have absolutely zero plans to become one. But take a closer look at the character qualities in the passage. You'll notice that what's really listed here is the type of character that all followers of Jesus ought to show. You don't get a pass just because you're not in official church leadership.

The best way to build good character is to start early by developing good habits. Build spiritual disciplines into your life like Scripture memorization, prayer, and Bible study. These habits will help you build the type of character Paul talks about in today's passage. And who knows, perhaps God will one day use you in leadership in a local church.

Start by memorizing the verse on pages 38-39 of this book.

As you pray, focus on three key areas. First, ask God to help you develop good character. Invite Him to show you areas of your life that need some character work. Second, pray for those currently in leadership in your local church. They are in challenging roles and you can encourage them simply by praying regularly for them. Finally, ask God to raise up new people to serve as leaders in the church who are people of character.

The Key to Character

discover

READ 1 TIMOTHY 3:14-16.

**And most certainly, the mystery of godliness is great:
He was manifested in the flesh, vindicated in the
Spirit, seen by angels, preached among the nations,
believed on in the world, taken up in glory.
— 1 Timothy 3:16**

Paul had just finished laying out the character standard for church leadership, which is really the standard we're all called to as followers of Jesus. In today's passage, he pointed us to the ultimate model for our character which is found in the person of Jesus. The temptation in trying to build up our character is to simply do it ourselves. We want to just put in more effort and "try harder."

The reality is that trying harder can often lead to us feeling like failures. A better approach is to look at our focus. A great way to see this is by thinking about someone driving a car. A person driving can't keep all their focus on what's immediately in front of them or they'll miss what is coming down the road. Instead, the driver has to look in front of them and down the road, which leads to driving and breaking smoothly.

In the same way, if we keep our attention focused only on every small action right in front of us we will sometimes struggle more than we'd expect to. Instead, we ought to look further down the road to Jesus as our model for godliness. He is the ultimate example of godliness and the only source for building godliness and character into our own lives.

delight

What are some ways Jesus displayed godliness for us?

Why does character in the church matter?

display

If you want to focus on Jesus as the model for godly living, you need to understand specifically how He lived out that character in His life. Take some time to skim through Matthew, Mark, Luke, and John, and find places that show Jesus's character in action. Jot down those godly character traits Jesus displayed. Keep that list somewhere you can see it and to add to it as you continue to study God's Word. Pick a characteristic of godliness that you see in Jesus and focus today on living that same way through your actions.

Ask God in your prayer time to help you see the godly character Jesus displayed while living on earth. Thank God that you have a clear example in Jesus of what godliness looks like. Express your desire to God to live out your character in a Christlike way.

Truth vs. Lies

discover

READ 1 TIMOTHY 4:1-5.

Now the Spirit explicitly says that in later times some will depart from the faith, paying attention to deceitful spirits and the teachings of demons, through the hypocrisy of liars whose consciences are seared.
— 1 Timothy 4:1-2

We live in a culture where lies are constantly thrown our way. You see lies every day in advertising, on social media, and possibly even from your friends. Paul recognized that lies would even hit the church itself. He describes these lies as demonic and coming from people who couldn't even recognize right from wrong anymore. The lies he talked about created extra rules for Christians in some sort of attempt to be more spiritual.

How do we identify the lies and keep them from taking hold in our hearts? The best way to fight a lie is by shining the light of truth on it. We can see lies clearly when we walk faithfully with God because He is good and everything He created is good. We can fight against lies when we compare them to the truth of God's Word. We can know deep in our hearts the truth when we spend time in prayer asking God to show us the difference between truths and lies. Clinging to the truth will keep us faithfully following Jesus for a lifetime.

delight

In this passage, what were the liars listening to instead of God's truth?

Why is God's Word and prayer so important to knowing the truth?

display

Have you ever taken time to think through any lies you might believing? Use this opportunity today to look inside your heart and reflect. Think about areas where you might be tempted to believe lies instead of truth. These might be lies about yourself that you find yourself pulled to. They might be lies about God and His plans. They might be lies about your parents or other older mentors in your life. For each lie you recognize, identify a truth that you can replace it with. Make a decision to believe truth instead of lies.

Spend your time in prayer thanking God for the good gifts He has given you. Thank Him for salvation, spiritual maturity, and the ability to fight temptation. Thank Him for your family and friends. Thank Him for the good gift of a home to live in and food to eat. Close your time of prayer by committing to go through your day with this same attitude of gratitude.

Training for Godliness

discover

READ 1 TIMOTHY 4:6-10.

For the training of the body has limited benefit, but godliness is beneficial in every way, since it holds promise for the present life and also for the life to come.
— 1 Timothy 4:8

I decided to play football my freshman year of high school. Prior to this, I had never played football before except for in the front yard of my house. The football season began with practices two times a day during the hottest month of the year. We ran and ran. We climbed up and down picnic tables. We did drills through old tires, and we did more push-ups than I care to remember. All that physical training was for the goal of getting us ready to compete on the football field.

Physical training is great, but it's limited. As Christians, we can sometimes put a tremendous amount of effort into readying ourselves for sports teams, artistic endeavors, or academic interests. Yet, we forget that it's even more important to train ourself for godliness. Training for godliness is the best type of training because it helps us out right now in our daily lives, and it helps us in the life we'll one day live when we're with Jesus for eternity.

Like Paul said, there is some benefit to physical training, but it's not eternal. Are you putting more effort into training that lasts or training that doesn't?

delight

How do good teaching and words of the faith nourish you?

Why is training for godliness so important?

Character and Courage

display

We don't love the word *discipline* but it's a reality we need. If you want to succeed on a sports team, it's going to take discipline. If you want to grow in godliness, it's going to take discipline. Christians since the time of Jesus have practiced different spiritual disciplines such as reading the Bible, silence and solitude, and prayer. The fact that you're reading these words right now means that you are pursuing spiritual disciplines in your life.

But what's next? Is there a spiritual discipline you can add to your life that might help you grow in godliness more? It might be journaling, serving others, or meditating on Scripture. Pick a discipline today that you can start to learn more about and put into practice.

One way to grow in the spiritual discipline of prayer is by being intentional in how you pray. Format your prayer time today by using the four parts of prayer in the acronym ACTS. Adoration—worshiping God for who He is and what He has done. Confession—being honest with God about specific sin in your life and repenting of it. Thanksgiving—demonstrating your gratitude to God. Supplication—asking God to meet your needs and the needs of others.

Set an Example

discover

READ 1 TIMOTHY 4:11–5:2.

Don't let anyone despise your youth, but set an example for the believers in speech, in conduct, in love, in faith, and in purity.
— 1 Timothy 4:12

Has someone ever completely written you off because of your age? Maybe you've had security guards give you mean looks while you're hanging out with your friends at the mall. Maybe you've tried to participate in conversation with older family members and felt like your thoughts and opinions didn't matter. Or maybe you've tried to serve in a ministry but felt like you were overlooked because you're seen as not old enough.

Timothy likely wasn't quite as young as you are, but as a young pastor he received some great advice from his mentor. Paul told Timothy to not let anyone look down on him because of his age. It's easy sometimes to simply feel like we've got nothing to contribute at a young age. But our response ought to be different. Instead of feeling overlooked, choose to set an example.

Paul gives five areas to set an example in—the way you talk, the way you act, the way you love, the way you believe, and the way you honor God. You can make an incredible difference when you decide to grow up in these areas instead of giving up when overlooked.

delight

Why do you think Paul mentioned these five areas to set an example in?

Why do you think Paul gave specific instructions for how to treat believers of different ages?

display

It can be tempting to think you should just wait to live fully for Christ until you're older, but God wants to do incredible things through your life right now. Pick one of the areas Paul challenged Timothy to set an example in and make an intentional effort to grow in that area. For example, maybe focus this week on making your speech an example for other believers. This might mean choosing to use words that honor God better or it might mean encouraging others with your words.

In your prayer time, ask God to reveal to you areas of your life where you can set an example right now. Seek to discover areas of sin that need to be dealt with. Ask Him to show you opportunities to live out this life as an example to others. Humble yourself as you pray by recognizing it's not about bringing attention to yourself; it's about humbly helping others see how to follow Jesus more closely.

MEMORY
VERSE

Don't let anyone despise
your youth, but set
an example for the
believers in speech,
in conduct, in love, in
faith, and in purity.

— 1 Timothy 4:12

Meet Real Needs

discover

READ 1 TIMOTHY 5:3-16.

Support widows who are genuinely in need.
— 1 Timothy 5:3

The world we live in is full of people in need. There are people in need of housing, people in need of food, and people just in need of someone to show care and concern. In my city, I can't drive more than a mile or two without seeing someone asking for money at stop lights. It's a reality of our modern times, but knowing how to best meet the need of someone who is hurting can be a challenge.

Paul gave Timothy specific instructions for how to care for the widows in his church community. We can learn big picture principles from these instructions for how to care for the vulnerable and hurting all around us. We may be tempted to respond to requests for help with one of two extremes. The first extreme is to attempt to help everyone we encounter. This approach isn't sustainable for everyone, could be dangerous at times, and maybe isn't always the wisest approach. The second extreme is to never help anyone. This approach seems to miss the heart of Jesus which deeply cared for those in pain.

Paul challenged Timothy to wisely care for those who were in genuine need. We ought to pursue the same goal as we seek to help those who are hurting.

delight

Who does Paul say should primarily be the first resource for caring for widows? Why is this important?

What are some general principles you can take away from this passage and how to help those in need?

When can it be unwise or unsafe to help those who are hurting?

display

The local church isn't just a place for Christians to gather and learn. It's also designed to be a community that cares for the hurting and vulnerable living nearby. Look for opportunities through your local church to minister to those who are vulnerable and in need. If those opportunities don't exist, see if you can find time to talk with your pastor or youth leader about how your church might be able to show the love of Jesus to others by meeting needs. Some areas you might explore include local soup kitchens, crisis pregnancy centers, or groups that provide shelter and housing for those in need.

Pray for God to give you a greater heart for those who are in need. Ask Him to help you have the same heart He does for them. Seek God's wisdom as you look to meet needs and to lead you to wise adults who are able to help you minister to those around you.

Bad News/Good News

discover

READ 1 TIMOTHY 5:17-25.

**Likewise, good works are obvious, and those that
are not obvious cannot remain hidden.
— 1 Timothy 5:25**

Have you ever disobeyed your parents and pretended like it never happened, just wishing and hoping they would never find out? Most of the time, parents figure it out. They quickly see through what's going on. On the other hand, do you sometimes wish they would discover the hidden good things you do too?

In our moments of weakness, we might want to brag about the good stuff we've done that others had no clue about. "Mom, I brushed and flossed every day this week." Or, "Dad, I took out the trash and no one even noticed." Or, "Did you guys even see that I made dinner for myself and my siblings?"

Here's some bad news and some good news. The bad stuff we do is all going to come out in the end. No matter how much we try to hide it, God knows and will bring it to light. But here's the good news: the good things we do in secret will also come to light. We don't need to brag about them, post them on our social media story, or print a t-shirt letting everyone know how great we've been. God will honor us at just the right time, and He will receive the glory which is really what it's all about.

delight

What are some ways we can honor those in church leadership?

Take a quick look at Matthew 5:16. How does that help you better understand today's passage?

display

Our world is all about self-promotion. We're quick to call attention to ourselves and our accomplishments. Today, dare to be different. Be on the lookout for ways you can do good to others without them noticing. Come up with at least five things you can do in the near future that will be good for others but won't lead to you getting any credit or praise for it. Bless people in your life but actively attempt to avoid any sort of recognition for it. Do something kind for your parents but try not to let them know it was you who did it.

Start your prayer time by expressing your thankfulness to God for the reality that it's not all about you. Praise Him that He will be the one to get the glory for good works in your life. Ask Him to show you any hidden sin that needs to come into the light by confessing it to God. Close your time by asking Him to help you see opportunities to do good works.

Respect for Everyone

discover

READ 1 TIMOTHY 6:1-2.

Let those who have believing masters not be disrespectful to them because they are brothers, but serve them even better, since those who benefit from their service are believers and dearly loved.
— 1 Timothy 6:2

Passages like this one can be tough to read with our modern minds because we tend to think about slavery in the context of American history. Two things are important to remember when you read about slavery in the Bible. First, slavery in the Bible was not race-based as it has been in our own history. Second, the Bible never condones slavery but instead gives instructions for how those existing relationships in society were supposed to operate. Paul was giving Timothy instructions here for how slaves ought to handle their relationships with their masters who were also Christians.

From these verses we can walk away with some principles for how to treat others. Our respect for others, particularly if they're in positions of authority over us, reveals our respect for God. We might think that our relationship with God is only about Him and us. However, followers of Jesus display their love for God in the way they treat people. So, it's important for us to love others—both believers and non-believers—for their own benefit and to reflect our respect for God.

It is also important to make it abundantly clear that if someone is hurting you, showing them respect does not mean you allow them to continue hurting you. If you are in a relationship or situation where someone is causing you harm, seek help. In this situation, it is important to show respect for yourself and get the help you need.

delight

What are some specific examples of people believers should show respect for?

Why does Paul encourage people to show even more respect to people who are believers?

display

Our culture loves to tear people down. Every day, you are faced with opportunities to respect others instead of showing disrespect. Imagine the difference you can make with those you influence if you just decided to respect people in a different way than most others do. List out some people you sometimes struggle to show respect. This list might include parents, certain teachers, or even friends. Next to each name, write down one practical way you can increase the respect you show that person. Over the next week, seek to show respect to those people through the ideas you wrote down.

Search your heart to see if you have been showing disrespect to others. Start first by asking God to show you how you've disrespected those who don't know Jesus. Next, ask God to show you how you may have shown disrespect to other believers. Take this opportunity to repent of disrespect, accept Jesus's forgiveness for it, and commit to move forward with a new attitude of respect.

True Contentment

discover

READ 1 TIMOTHY 6:3-10.

**For the love of money is a root of all kinds of evil, and
by craving it, some have wandered away from the
faith and pierced themselves with many griefs.
— 1 Timothy 6:10**

Everyone is chasing something. Some people chase popularity, others
chase the highest GPA, and others chase happiness. However, one
of the most dangerous things to chase is money. Money is necessary
to live, so it's not evil in and of itself. But we must be careful to avoid
making money the main pursuit of our lives. You might not think this is
a huge issue as a teenager since you may not have a lot of money, but
possessions and money can be a subtle trap that quickly takes us over.

The chase for contentment is a much better pursuit. Contentment
isn't lazy, but it recognizes the difference between needs and wants.
Contentment is only found in Jesus. It is why someone like the apostle
Paul could write from prison "for I have learned to be content in
whatever circumstances I find myself. I know how to make do with little,
and I know how to make do with a lot. In any and all circumstances I
have learned the secret of being content—whether well fed or hungry,
whether in abundance or in need. I am able to do all things through him
who strengthens me" (Phil. 4:11b-13). The One who gave Paul strength
to be content in any situation is the same One who strengthens you—the
Lord Jesus Christ.

delight

Describe a time when you have seen someone's pursuit of something become unhealthy for them.

Paul reminded Timothy that we can't take anything with us when we die. So, how do we balance our wants and needs in everyday life?

display

The best way to chase after contentment is by showing gratitude for what you have. Have you ever received gifts at a party and your parents made you write thank-you notes to everyone who gave you a gift? Writing those notes can get tiring, but today's a great day to write a thank-you note to God. Grab something to write with and let Him know how grateful you are for all He's blessed you with. If you're not sure where to start, begin by thinking about where you live—the roof over your head, the people you live with, and the place you get to sleep. Those things are probably not all perfect, but when you say thank you, it helps you experience contentment.

Take that thank-you note you just wrote and turn it into a prayer. If you're able, read your note out loud to God. If that feels weird, take a few minutes to slowly read it silently as a prayer to God. As you pray through the note, thank God for other things that may come to your mind.

The Good Fight

discover

READ 1 TIMOTHY 6:11-16.

**But you, man of God, flee from these things, and pursue righteousness, godliness, faith, love, endurance, and gentleness.
— 1 Timothy 6:11**

The apostle Paul wrote a lot of the New Testament, and there's so much to love about his writings. One thing I love is how he never tells Christians to stop doing something without telling them to start doing something else. Have you ever tried to stop a bad habit merely by focusing on not doing it? It's nearly impossible. It's much easier to stop a bad habit by replacing it with a good habit.

That's exactly what Paul told Timothy to focus on here. He told Timothy to flee from things like false doctrine, fighting, and the love of money. Then, he also told Timothy what to focus on instead. Paul gave Timothy a target to shoot for, and his instructions apply to us today as well. We can truly grow in our relationship with Jesus when we flee from what's evil and pursue the things of God instead.

delight

Why would Paul single out the six things he told Timothy to pursue in 1 Timothy 6:11? (Hint: Read Galatians 5:22-23.)

What do you think it means to fight the good fight of the faith?

display

The word "pursue" indicates much more than a casual effort. A pursuit requires energy, intentionality, and focus. If you're hoping to grow in your walk with Jesus, you need those things as well. Take a look at the six elements listed in verse 11 and pick just one to focus on. Now, come up with a plan for how you will pursue the thing you picked. Are there Bible verses you'll memorize? Someone you'll ask to hold you accountable? A book to read? Take the first steps today to pursue these things in a new way.

In your prayer time, use the last part of today's passage (vv. 15b-16) to help you worship God by focusing on specific attributes. Praise Him for His role as King of kings and Lord of lords. Rest in awe of the fact that He is immortal. Consider what it means for Jesus to live in unapproachable light. Finally, declare to Him that He's worthy of honor and eternal power.

True Riches

discover

READ 1 TIMOTHY 6:17-21.

Instruct them to do what is good, to be rich in good works, to be generous and willing to share, storing up treasure for themselves as a good foundation for the coming age, so that they may take hold of what is truly life.
— 1 Timothy 6:18-19

It's not a sin to be rich, but those who are rich need to be careful how they use their resources. The problem with wealth arises when hope is placed on riches and material things instead of God.

As a teenager, it can be easy to put hope in the reactions you get on social media, praise from teachers, or being in a dating relationship. A better option is to find true riches by investing in the actions of good works. These investments pay off for eternity instead of the present day where it truly won't last.

This first letter from Paul to Timothy has been full of incredible wisdom and instruction. Paul closed it by challenging Timothy to keep a close guard on that instruction and on the gift God gave him as a young pastor. Consider this advice to be words that apply to you as well. You are not a pastor, but you can seek character and wisdom and to use well the gifts God has given you. These are the things that lead to true, lasting, and eternal wealth.

delight

Why is it important to not be arrogant about riches or put hope in wealth?

What are some examples of good works that store up treasure for the age to come?

display

Your walk with Jesus is either moving forward or moving backward. It won't ever move forward by accident. You have to take the initiative to move it forward. Just as Paul told Timothy to guard what was entrusted to him, you can do the same. Take time today to reflect on the essentials of your faith. Remind yourself the importance of knowing Jesus through the gospel. Let yourself rest in the reality of who you are in Christ.

As you pray, ask God to remind you of what you need to cling to and guard. Ask Him to remind you through the Holy Spirit of the truth He has shown you in His Word. Pray that He would give you opportunities to strengthen other believers in their faith. Submit your desires to Him as you start what's next for you.

Character and Courage

COURAGE

SECTION 2

Sometimes we think of people from the Bible as superheroes. Truth be told, they were normal people just like us with struggles, temptations, and fears. They had to rely on the Holy Spirit just like we do. Thankfully, the Holy Spirit who empowered them, is the same Holy Spirit who gives us courage today to follow where He leads and to live in the truth of His Word.

A Simple Greeting

discover

READ 1 TIMOTHY 1:1-2.

Paul, an apostle of Christ Jesus by God's will, for the sake of the promise of life in Christ Jesus.
— 2 Timothy 1:1

You probably don't think much about how a letter starts. It's usually something like "Dear So-and-So" or maybe it just jumps right in. In fact, we don't spend much time on greetings at all since most of our communication happens through text message. But the beginning of a letter can tell us a lot about the author and the audience. This second letter to Timothy is a big deal because it's the last letter we have from Paul.

Think about what we can pick up from just this short greeting. Paul identified himself as an apostle of Jesus. An apostle was someone who knew Jesus personally and functioned as His messenger. (Acts 9 shows us that Paul got to know Jesus up close and personal while traveling to Damascus.) The apostles set the foundation of teaching and life for the young church that was absolutely essential. Ultimately, Paul truly gave his life for the sake of the gospel.

The investment of Paul's life for the gospel is illustrated perfectly by the person receiving this letter—Timothy. Paul modeled the life for Timothy that we're called to pursue today as well.

delight

What does Paul's greeting tell us about this letter to Timothy?

Why do you think the promise of life in Christ Jesus motivated Paul so much?

Character and Courage

display

It can be helpful sometimes to picture what you hope the end of the story looks like. Paul wrote this incredible last letter to Timothy at the end of what had been an amazing life of living for the sake of the gospel rather than for himself. Have you ever thought about what you want your life story to look like at the very end? It's easy to get caught up in what classes you're taking next year or what you'll be doing for fun this weekend instead of truly dreaming about how you hope the future goes.

In two or three sentences, describe how you want your walk with Jesus to look like when you reach the end of life's journey. Paint a picture with your words of how you hope to finish well.

As you spend some time in prayer, ask God to show you how to live a life that is truly centered on the gospel. Surrender your own desires to His desires. Ask Him to show you how to take one small step today that will move you into further obedience to Jesus.

Courageous Living

discover

READ 2 TIMOTHY 1:3-7.

For God has not given us a spirit of fear, but one of power, love, and sound judgment.
— 2 Timothy 1:7

People have fears about all sorts of things in life. Some people are scared of heights, darkness, or small spaces. Other people have more unique fears such as being scared of clowns or mimes. In fact, just reading the word "fear" may immediately bring your personal fears to mind.

The good news is that God doesn't intend for us to be ruled by fear. In fact, Paul wrote that the spirit God gives isn't one of fear at all, but instead it's one of power, love, and sound judgment. You might think courage is all about never experiencing the emotion of fear, bur courage doesn't mean you'll never be afraid of anything. Instead, courage is choosing to live in the power, love, and sound judgment God gives you when fear shows its ugly face.

It's possible that Timothy may have needed a little boost of encouragement at this point in his ministry. Maybe he was feeling a little beat up by everything the world had thrown at him. Paul knew exactly what he needed to hear. Timothy needed the reminder that fear can be overcome because of God's work in our lives.

delight

How does a person pray constantly as Paul said he prayed for Timothy?

What's different between a spirit of fear and a spirit of power, love, and sound judgment?

display

What scares you? Are you letting fear drive your life more than faith? All of us face things in life that bring fear. The key is remembering the resources God has given you. Take some practical action on the fears you may be facing. First, identify the fear you're dealing with. Write it down or say it out loud. Next, think through each of the three items Paul encouraged Timothy with and answer these questions:

What would it look like to experience power over your fear?

How can love drive out your fear?

How can you exercise sound judgment over your fear?

Use your time of prayer to ask God to give you freedom from fear. Be honest with Him about the fears you face. Ask for courage in dealing with these fears. Allow God to remind you that it's not about you putting on a brave face—it's about trusting in His resources more than you trust in your fear.

Generous Grace

discover

READ 2 TIMOTHY 1:8-12.

He has saved us and called us with a holy calling, not according to our works, but according to his own purpose and grace, which was given to us in Christ Jesus before time began.
— 2 Timothy 1:9

I attended a very small middle school and my entire eighth grade class had the opportunity to take a Spring field trip to visit Washington, DC. We were able to see firsthand what we had been studying that whole year. We had to earn the trip though. The first requirement was to pass a test on the United States Constitution. We had to know the basics of what it said and had to memorize all the amendments. The second requirement was financial. We had to either pay or raise the funds to go on the trip. I still remember selling tickets to a giant spaghetti dinner in our school gym. The trip was incredible and felt like a great reward for our hard work.

Some people view salvation the same as my eighth grade field trip. They think they'll earn salvation if they work hard enough, put the effort into the right things, and pay whatever the cost will be. Aren't you glad that's not how God operates with us? He saves us, not because of our works, but because it's part of His purpose to fully wash us in His amazing grace. It's a gift that's waiting for each of us to receive.

delight

Why is it a big deal that salvation is only from God's grace and not our good works?

Read back over verse 12. What encourages you about how Jesus guards our salvation?

Character and Courage

display

Paul gave us a couple of clear points of action in this passage relating to the salvation we've freely received. First, we're to share in suffering for the gospel. Take some time to research how Christians are persecuted throughout the world by using a website like persecution.com.

Second, we're to live without shame for our faith. This can be difficult during your teenage years because how others see you can feel like a really big deal. Focus instead on how God sees you. He's not ashamed to call you His child so you can be unashamed to call Him your heavenly Father and to help point others to salvation.

In your prayer time, thank God that you didn't have to earn your salvation. Express your gratitude that it's a free gift of grace. Pray specifically for Christians who are enduring suffering, whether you know them personally or have learned about those living in a different place. Ask God to give you boldness through the power of His Spirit as you seek to live unashamed for Him.

DAY 20

Holding On

discover

READ 2 TIMOTHY 1:13-18.

Hold on to the pattern of sound teaching that you have heard from me, in the faith and love that are in Christ Jesus.
— 2 Timothy 1:13

I've always been fascinated by animals that can blend into their surroundings. You've probably seen snakes that look like the dirt they slither across, chameleons that match the plants around them, or bugs that look like sticks and love to hang out on trees. They're pretty cool to see. However, have you ever thought about how we sometimes function the same way?

Let's face it. The world we live in values a lot of things that are different than what God values and has shown us in the Bible. Paul recognized that Timothy had a choice: he could be swayed by the surrounding cultural values or he could choose to hold on to the sound teaching he'd received from Paul. After all, he'd seen other people walk away from the faith when things got tough. We're faced with the same challenge as Timothy.

It's easy to become like the culture we live in, but it takes focused effort to hold strong to the truth that we're taught in Scripture. Sound teaching will keep us grounded during the challenges life brings our way.

Character and Courage

delight

What are some of the basic truths that would be part of the "sound teaching" Paul wrote about?

What differences do you see between the two people Paul mentioned in verse 15 and the man he mentioned in verse 16?

display

Here are three super practical ways you can hold on to sound teaching. First, listen to or watch good Bible teaching. There are incredible resources out there to help you understand the Bible better. Make sure to listen well and take notes when your pastor preaches. Second, read a little bit of the Bible every day. The fact that you're reading this right now means you're already off to a great start in making daily Bible reading a lifelong habit!

Finally, memorize the Scriptures. Start small and pick verses that are meaningful to you. You might write them on note cards or keep them in a note-taking app on your phone. As long as you regularly review the verses you're memorizing, you'll be able to keep them in your heart and bring them quickly to your mind. Go ahead and memorize the verses on pages 72-73.

As you talk to God in prayer, ask Him to give you strength to hold on to sound teaching. Acknowledge the things in your life that sometimes seem to distract you from this teaching. Ask God to remind you of what He has already shown you in His Word. Ask Him to surround you with people who will encourage you in holding on to sound teaching.

MEMORY VERSE

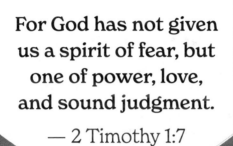

For God has not given us a spirit of fear, but one of power, love, and sound judgment.

— 2 Timothy 1:7

DAY 21

Pass It On

discover

READ 2 TIMOTHY 2:1-7.

What you have heard from me in the presence of many witnesses, commit to faithful men who will be able to teach others also.
— 2 Timothy 2:2

Every one of us walks through life with knowledge someone else passed on to us. My parents taught me how to brush my teeth, ride a bike, and tie my shoes. Practical pieces of information like these are things you'll one day pass on to the next generation as well.

Paul wanted Timothy to think of his faith as not just something that he kept to himself. Paul challenged Timothy to pass that faith on and encouraged a perspective that didn't look to just one step past Timothy, but actually two steps beyond. Timothy was to look for people who would not just receive the faith but would also pass it on to others.

It's easy to think about our faith as something that's just of personal benefit. But Paul challenges us to keep a bigger view in mind. We need to see our faith as something that continually flows through us and into others who will then pass that faith onto others.

delight

Why is it so important that faith passes on to generations beyond our own?

Notice the three examples Paul gives in verses 3-6. What do they all have in common? How does this apply to our faith?

display

It's easy to become self-centered, only thinking about ourselves. We can even do this with our faith when we enjoy how our relationship with God gives us strength and peace. Think of someone in your life to whom you might be able to pass on some of your faith to. This might be a younger sibling, someone in your student ministry at church, or a friend at school. Now, pick one thing God has been showing you recently through the Bible that you can share with that person. Don't be preachy about it or act like you're better; simply share what God has been showing you and ask that person for his or her thoughts.

As you pray today, ask God to show you people who you can pass your faith on to and specific things from His Word that you can share with these people. Then, ask God to help you live with the focus of a soldier, athlete, and farmer.

Faithful

discover

READ 2 TIMOTHY 2:8-13.

If we are faithless, he remains faithful, for he cannot deny himself.
— 2 Timothy 2:13

It can be tempting for some people to treat the act of becoming a Christian as something you do and then you move on with your life. Paul reminded Timothy that he was to remember Jesus. I don't think this means Timothy was forgetful, but it's an encouragement to always keep Jesus at the front of his mind. We can get distracted by so many things in life and forget about what's truly important.

The mark of people who belong to Jesus is that their lives will change to look more and more like Jesus over time. People who have truly been saved will endure until the end. Paul recognized this and worked hard to help Christians stay faithful for the long haul. The good news about faithfulness is that our salvation is ultimately dependent on the faithfulness of Jesus, not our own. Jesus is faithful even when we are not because it is a part of His character, which He cannot deny.

It's the faithfulness of Jesus that enables us to be faithful. You can't maintain your salvation in your own strength. He gives us the strength to be courageous, faithful, unashamed, and fully committed to Him.

delight

What are things you can do to help you "remember" as Paul encouraged Timothy to do in verse 8?

We are called to endure and not deny Jesus. How can we choose to endure, even if it means suffering, instead of denying Him?

display

You may be facing some difficult situations in life right now. You might even feel like you don't know how you're going to make it through. Rest today in the fact that Jesus will give you the courage and strength you need to endure. Following Jesus is challenging, but it's also something we always do in His strength, not our own. You may not feel like having faith today but trust in Jesus to supply you the faith you need. Choose today to deny yourself and live for Christ in every area of your life.

In your prayer time, confess to God any areas where you may have been struggling to remain faithful. Ask Him to give you the strength to endure difficult times and to give you the ability to trust Him in a deeper way. Thank Him for His faithful character and the way He has displayed it in your life.

Character and Courage

No Shame

discover

READ 2 TIMOTHY 2:14-19.

Be diligent to present yourself to God as one approved, a worker who doesn't need to be ashamed, correctly teaching the word of truth.
— 2 Timothy 2:15

Have you ever heard of a little white lie? It's one of those lies where it may not seem like a big deal at first, and you might even think it's not really hurting anyone. But what often happens is you end up having to constantly keep track of your story and possibly tell more lies in order to keep it going.

A dishonest life leads to having to always watch your back for fear of getting caught. More importantly, being dishonest runs contrary to the life of character God has called us to live. Paul challenged Timothy to live a life of truthfulness. He encouraged Timothy to live a life open and honest before God where he didn't have to be ashamed. The proper teaching of truth leads to this unashamed life.

The word of truth that Timothy taught is the same word of truth that all Christians are to place as the guiding direction for their lives. There is an incredible amount of noise in this world we live in. The key to navigating the noise is listening to and applying the truth of Scripture in our lives.

delight

Why is false teaching a danger we ought to avoid? How can we learn to identify what is false teaching?

What comfort do you find in verse 19?

display

Timothy had regular opportunities to teach the truth of Scripture to others in his ministry as a pastor. You probably do not have the same opportunities as Timothy, but you can set a great starting point for yourself by embracing the truth of Scripture instead of the lies of our culture. Memorize this short phrase: "What does the Bible say?" Make this the question you ask every time you encounter something that claims to be true.

A second way you can display this teaching is by passing on truth to others. You may not be a pastor, but you have people in your life who look up to you. Find a small nugget of biblical truth you can share with someone else this week and then take the opportunity to do it.

As you pray, ask God to help you live centered in His truth so you can live a life that's unashamed. Search your heart to see if there are any areas of your life that are out of line with the teachings of the Bible. Ask God to help you live obediently in any areas He reveals to you.

Youthful Passions

discover

READ 2 TIMOTHY 2:20-26.

Flee from youthful passions, and pursue righteousness, faith, love, and peace, along with those who call on the Lord from a pure heart.
— 2 Timothy 2:22

I loved watching cartoons as a kid. I remember one day asking my mom if she liked cartoons, and she told me that she didn't. I couldn't believe it! How could someone not like cartoons? Now, years later, I get it. There are some things that belong to childhood and other things that belong to adulthood.

The season of life you're in is full of all sorts of desires that seek to draw your attention. Paul recognized this in his letter to Timothy. He urged him to not just try to avoid youthful passions if he could but to flee from those passions.

Fortunately, as Paul usually did, he gave some things to replace those youthful passions with. He used a very active word in "flee" for the thing to avoid and then another active word in "pursue" as he told Timothy what to chase. We're to pursue righteousness, faith, love, and peace. The good news is it's pretty tough to continue chasing youthful passions if all your energy is going toward pursuing these other things instead.

delight

What is the value of setting yourself apart for God to use you?

How can someone strive to pursue the good things Paul mentioned instead of youthful passions?

display

Paul talked about four traits in this passage that we ought to pursue—righteousness, faith, love, and peace. Pick one of these four traits that you'd like to make an intentional effort to pursue. Once you've identified something to pursue, create an action plan for how you'll pursue it. Choose three actions to be part of your action plan. You might choose some Bible verses to memorize, a conversation to have with a leader at church, or a Bible study to work through with some friends. The effort you put into this pursuit will also help you avoid sin and temptation.

Take time to pray about the character trait you've decided to pursue. Ask God to empower you through the Holy Spirit to live in the way He desires you to. Surrender your desires to Him and ask Him to replace those with His desires.

Character and Courage

Take Courage

discover

READ 2 TIMOTHY 3:1-9.

**But know this: Hard times will come in the last days.
— 2 Timothy 3:1**

After Jesus died and was raised from the dead, He spent a brief period of time with His disciples. Then, He ascended into heaven but not before promising His disciples He would return one day. The last days can be viewed as the entire period between Jesus's first coming and second coming. He predicted it would get worse and worse. Paul laid out how true this is. The list of how people would live in the last days is pretty long and, if you think about it, sounds a lot like the times we live in today.

So, what should we do as we encounter people like this? Paul urges us to avoid these people. The reality is we become like those we spend time with. The subtle influence of people around us can be quite surprising. Our goal, then, is to stand strong and to take courage in what God has done in us. We can seek to become more influential to the people around us than they are on us. This only happens when we surround ourselves with solid, godly community and immerse ourselves in God's Word.

delight

Which types of people on Paul's list surprise you?

According to verses 6-9, what can happen when these types of people make their way into places of influence with people inside the church?

Character and Courage

display

The key to avoiding bad influences is to surround yourself with good influences. Who do you have in your life that is helping you follow Jesus closer? Draw a circle and put your name in the middle of it. Surround your name with people in your life who serve as godly influences on you. Make sure to include family members, people at church, and Christian friends at school. Do you feel like you have enough godly influences surrounding you? If not, think of strong Christians you know and make a plan to spend more time with them this week.

As you pray today, ask God to protect you from those in this world who would tear you down. Ask Him to surround you with people who build you up in faith. Tell God specific areas of your life you'd like to have strength and courage in. Rest in the reality that He is in control of the world around you.

The Bible's Purpose

discover

READ 2 TIMOTHY 3:10-17.

All Scripture is inspired by God and is profitable for teaching, for rebuking, for correcting, for training in righteousness, so that the man of God may be complete, equipped for every good work.
— 2 Timothy 3:16-17

Paul packed a lot of meaning about the role of the Bible into these two short verses at the end of today's passage. First, he talked about Scripture being inspired by God. This is different than being inspired to write a piece of poetry or a book. It carries the idea of God Himself breathing the Scripture through the human authors He used to write it.

Second, Paul gave four items the Bible is helpful for. The Bible shows us what to believe (teaching), how not to live (rebuking), what not to believe (correcting), and how to live (training in righteousness).[1] In other words, the Bible addresses every area of the Christian life.

Finally, Paul demonstrated that the purpose of Scripture is to bring us to maturity so that we will be ready for every good work God calls us to. God never intends for anyone to stay a baby Christian. The goal is to grow up in the faith. The Word of God, having a right understanding of it, and knowing it is a huge part of growing in our faith.

[1] Christopher W. Morgan and Robert A. Peterson, *Christian Theology: The Biblical Story and Our Faith* (Nashville, TN: B&H Academic, 2020), 64.

delight

When has the Bible taught you? Rebuked you? Corrected you? Trained you in righteousness?

How does the Bible being inspired by God make it different than other books, even Christian books?

display

It's sometimes easy to seek to live our Christian life by how we feel at the moment instead of the by the truth of Scripture. A better way is to let the Bible guide our feelings and actions. Take a few minutes to work through each purpose of Scripture and reflect on how you can put it into practice. Start with teaching, move to rebuking, shift over to correcting, and finish with training in righteousness. See if you can think of one way each of these concepts can help you as you read the Bible.

Teaching

Rebuking

Correcting

Training in Righteousness

Spend your prayer time thanking God for His Word. Focus on specific ways you have grown through reading the Bible. Meditate on how it has shaped you in your faith. Ask God to give you a greater desire to read and follow the Bible.

Be Ready

discover

READ 2 TIMOTHY 4:1-5.

Preach the word; be ready in season and out of season; correct, rebuke and encourage with great patience and teaching.
— 2 Timothy 4:2

I was on the basketball team for two years in middle school. Keep in mind, I was not a good basketball player; I was merely on the team. I wasn't a starter so I knew I wouldn't be on the court as the game got started. But my coach was fair and, sure enough, eventually he'd end up calling my name to get out on the court and play. A basketball player has to be ready to go into the game at any time. At any moment, I could be called up to get in the game and play my part, no matter how large or small it was.

Paul encouraged Timothy to be ready with the truth of God's Word at all times. God calls us to the same thing today even if you're not a pastor or overseas missionary. We live in a day when people are very interested in spiritual things, but ultimately many of them only want to hear what sounds good to them. God's Word can be tough to hear when it confronts areas of our lives that need adjustment. We must be ready to share it with others and ready to hear it ourselves at all times.

delight

What type of attitude should we have when correcting, rebuking, and encouraging? How do you know?

How do you see people turning away from the truth of Scripture? No matter how great or how small, what role can you play to help people turn toward God?

display

A basketball player stays ready for action by putting in the effort at practice and staying focused during the game. Are you putting in the effort of practice with God's Word? Select a Bible verse or two that you'd like to memorize. Spend the next few days committing it to memory so you'll be ready to use it when the time comes. See pages 104-105 to help you get started.

Are you staying focused during the everyday routine of life? Make a conscious effort to see the situations you face daily through the same eyes God sees them with. It's easy to coast through life, but you can choose to be ready to engage with God's Word when the opportunity comes up.

In your prayer time, ask God to give you a greater desire for truth. Ask for His protection from myths and false teachings that distract from the truth of the gospel. Thank God that He has revealed Himself through His Word and ask Him to help you discover more from it every day.

Finish Strong

discover

READ 2 TIMOTHY 4:6-8.

**I have fought the good fight, I have finished
the race, I have kept the faith.
— 2 Timothy 4:7**

It's tempting to slow down when you get to the end of something.
You've been working hard for hours on a school project, and you just
want to take a break. You've been running for miles, and you're ready
for a rest stop. You've been on your feet all day doing chores around the
house and you could really go for a nap. When you're incredibly close to
finishing, it's not the time to slow down. It's the time to push to the end
and finish strong!

Paul knew he was nearing the end of his life on earth, and he could
confidently say he'd given his all. A person can start running a race
strong, but what really matters is how they finish. Paul was determined
to finish well in a way that honored God and continued advancing
the gospel.

It's not enough for us to begin a relationship with Jesus in a passionate
way but lose our forward momentum as we go. God has called each one
of us to a lifelong pursuit of Jesus—always growing and moving forward.
As a disciple, you're called to finish strong.

delight

What did Paul mean when he said he was being poured out as a drink offering in 2 Timothy 4:6?

What does it look like for a Christian to finish well?

display

It can be helpful sometimes to do a little self-evaluation to check our progress as we follow Jesus. Answer the following questions on a scale of 1 to 10, with 1 being nope, 5 being sometimes, and 10 being for sure.

Am I more passionate today about my faith in Jesus than I was a year ago?

1   5   10

Do I regularly read God's Word?

1   5   10

Am I spending time in prayer (other than at meals)?

1   5   10

Do I seek to share the gospel with people who don't know Jesus?

1   5   10

Will the current state of your relationship with Jesus help move you toward the goal of finishing well? If it won't, make some changes today to have habits that will help you finish strong.

As you pray, ask God to reveal areas of your life where you may have started to slow down a bit spiritually. Ask Him to help you engage in spiritual disciplines in a fresh way. Ask Him to help you love those who don't know Jesus. Ask Him to surround you with people who will hold you accountable and help you finish strong.

DAY 29

Restored

discover

READ 2 TIMOTHY 4:9-15.

Only Luke is with me. Bring Mark with you, for
he is useful to me in the ministry.
— 2 Timothy 4:11

Friends can surprise us sometimes. True friendship usually shows up when we go through difficult times. And it's funny how sometimes the people we think will be right by our side seem to disappear when trouble comes. Sometimes it seems the people who do stick close to us are people we hadn't really thought would. Paul went through all sorts of issues with his friends in the ministry. Some stuck close and others abandoned him right in his moment of need.

Surprisingly, Mark was one of those guys who abandoned Paul. You can read about it in Acts 15:38, but it's interesting how things had changed at this point in Paul's ministry. Paul now saw Mark as useful to his ministry. If you'd only read about Mark earlier in Acts, you might think he was totally worthless. We can't ever fully write off anyone. God loves to redeem people from their mistakes and restore them to be used by Him again.

Paul had experienced abandonment in ministry, but he also got to experience the joy of seeing God bring partners in ministry, like Mark, back to be used again. Don't ever think God is done using someone. He just might surprise you.

delight

Who are the people who stick by you in the tough times? How can you show appreciation to them for their friendship?

When have you seen someone be restored after he or she made a serious mistake? How has God used that person's mistake for His glory?

display

Aren't you glad God doesn't give up on you? Even when you choose the wrong path, fall flat on your face, and experience deep failure, God is waiting to welcome you back and restore you as you repent.

Are there people in your life that you've written off as too far gone? Maybe you think they'll never come back to their faith. Perhaps you wonder if they'll ever be a godly friend again. Today, make the choice to believe the best about them. Try to see them the way God sees them— as His children who can be used in amazing ways. Pray for them and ask God to touch their hearts.

Pray today specifically for people who either you've written off or other people have written off. Ask God to give you a heart to see how He might use them in the future. See if the Holy Spirit might bring someone to mind who you can encourage this week with your words.

In God's Hands

discover

READ 2 TIMOTHY 4:16-22.

The Lord will rescue me from every evil work and will bring me safely into his heavenly kingdom. To him be the glory forever and ever! Amen.
— 2 Timothy 4:18

Have you ever gone hiking with a group and ended up behind everyone else? It can be a scary thing to be out in the woods and feel like you're all alone. Paul must have felt this way at times when people deserted him. In fact, in this passage, Paul shares how he was deserted by everyone at one point. But he held on to a firm reality. He knew God was on his side even if every human being around him was gone.

Paul gained his strength from the Lord when there was no human voice nearby to encourage him. He knew he was ultimately in God's hands. The incredible thing is that the safest place to be is in God's hands, even if you feel completely alone.

Paul recognized as he finished the work of his life and ministry that God would still be faithful to rescue him. Paul had been through a lot, but he understood there could be more challenges ahead! The final work God would complete would be to usher Paul into His kingdom. Paul's only response to this thought was to worship God and give Him all the glory.

delight

In verse 16, why do you think Paul hoped his companions' desertion wouldn't be counted against them?

What was the purpose of Paul being strengthened by the Lord?

display

Every single one of us faces loneliness and fear. It's so easy to feel like no one else cares or is there for you. If you're feeling this way, it's time to embrace two realities. The first reality is that there are people around you who are there for you even though you may not always believe it. The second reality is that God is always there for you and His presence is the most important one.

Write down one or two of your biggest fears. As you see that fear written out, remember that God will always be with you no matter what comes your way. He is faithful and will carry you through to the finish.

In your time of prayer, ask God to show you His strength in a clear way. Declare to Him that He is your only source of strength and power. Acknowledge that you can't follow Him apart from Him giving you the strength to do so. Surrender your fears and struggles to Him by naming them specifically and asking God for the strength to endure.

Memory Verse

All Scripture is
inspired by God
and is profitable
for teaching,
for rebuking,
for correcting,
for training in
righteousness, so
that the man of God
may be complete,
equipped for every
good work.

— 2 Timothy 3:16-17

NO ROOM FOR EXCUSES

As a student, you've probably said, "I'm not old enough yet," usually while wishfully thinking you were older. Though we might wish for the ages of drivers' licenses, high school graduations, or even being able to vote, the truth is these age limits exist as markers for maturity; they indicate the moments when we're considered mature enough to handle certain responsibilities. So, why did Paul tell Timothy, "Don't let anyone despise your youth, but set an example for the believers in speech, in conduct, in love, in faith, and in purity" (1 Tim. 4:12)?

Instead of using his age as an excuse—or doing things that allowed other people to use his age as an excuse—Paul encouraged Timothy to live above his age. In other words, age is not the standard, God is. No matter how old you are, there are things you can do right here and now to show others God's kingdom.

Think about it: What are some ways God has gifted you? Where has He placed you? What are you passionate about? God can use all of these things to help you show others who He is and why He's worth following.

Let's break this down. Each of these levels builds, going from things anyone can do at any age to things you might need special permission for or may need to be a bit older to do.

LEVEL 1: CONSIDER WHERE YOU LIVE AND INTERACT EVERY DAY.

What can you do at home to show your family—and people who regularly interact with your family—the love of Jesus?

What can you do at school to show the staff, volunteers, and your classmates the love of Jesus?

LEVEL 2: CONSIDER THE COMMUNITY AROUND YOU.

What group projects is your church or student ministry a part of? How can you join them?

What can your family do to show people in your neighborhood the love of Jesus?

LEVEL 3: CONSIDER NEEDS AROUND THE WORLD.

What mission trips does your church take each year that you look forward to being able to go on? If there's an age limit and you're old enough to go, what steps might you need to take to make it happen?

How can you pray for missionaries your church supports or missions trip members from your church?

No matter where you are or how old you are, you can always be doing something to spread the good news of God's kingdom and salvation in Jesus. So, what can you do now?

WHAT WILL YOU CHOOSE?

Maybe you've heard the idea that character is who you are when no one is watching. In simpler terms, character is a choice or the combination of choices spanning a lifetime. While salvation itself is a one-time yes, following Jesus by obeying God's Word is a daily—and sometimes moment-by-moment—decision. Every day, we face a multitude of choices that lead us to either follow the world and let our character deteriorate or follow God and see our character thrive.

Let's do a quick gut check. Circle or highlight the option that you'd be most tempted to choose.

- A friend asks you what you believe about something controversial and you know saying what you believe will upset them. Do you go with the flow to keep the peace or share what you believe, no matter the consequences?

- You aren't allowed go to prom unless you make at least an eighty on your final paper for English. You make a seventy-eight. Do you do some creative rounding and tell your parents you made an eighty so you can go or do you tell the truth and hope for leniency?

- You get pulled over for speeding. Do you tell your parents when you get home or figure out how to pay the ticket and not worry about it?

- Someone you admire says something awful about another person you know and admire. Do you agree, add something to it, say nothing, walk away, or stand up for your friend?

- The phone you've been wanting is finally on sale. You don't have the money saved up yet, but you know your older sibling has enough to cover it. You ask to borrow the amount and your sibling says no. Do you secretly take the cash and mentally promise to pay it back later or try to do extra work to earn the money to buy it yourself?

Now, look back at each scenario and consider one possible consequence for each option.

Sometimes, telling the truth doesn't give us what we want. Sometimes, we receive grace for telling the truth even when we've done wrong. When have you told a difficult truth and received grace?

What steps can you take to help you make more God-honoring choices more of the time? (Consider things like studying God's Word, surrounding yourself with godly friends, considering the consequences, etc.)

We're human, and the awful, beautiful truth is that humans aren't perfect, but God knows this. So, God offers us grace in Jesus. If you find yourself sliding into wrong choices and can't even remember how you got there, it's never too late to cry out to Him for forgiveness and help. God's grace is endless and boundless—He has more than enough grace to cover every one of our mistakes. All we have to do is ask.

What can you do when you make a choice you know is wrong?

Notes

Notes

Character and Courage

LIFEWAY STUDENT DEVOTIONS
Engage with God's Word.

lifeway.com/teendevotionals

☐ CALLED

☐ PRESENCE & PURPOSE

☐ REVEALED

☐ LION OF JUDAH

☐ YOUR WILL BE DONE

☐ SPIRIT & TRUTH

☐ THREE-IN-ONE

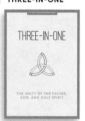

☐ IN THE BEGINNING

☐ TRUTH AND LOVE

☐ SEARCH AND KNOW

☐ TAKE UP AND FOLLOW

☐ THE SHEPHERD KING